CONTENTS

APPENDICES

CONTENTS

I

Foreword

The Report of the Select Committee on Scottish Affairs on *Land Resource Use in Scotland* (Session 1971–72), (Sub Committee A—Rural Land Use) recommended that the present regulations on muirburn should be examined and that the Nature Conservancy should consider, together with farmers and gamekeepers, means of promoting the best possible practice.

In Command Paper No. 5428 (Scottish Development Department—Government Observations on the Report of the Select Committee on Scottish Affairs) which followed publication of the Select Committee Report it was stated that the government would consult the Nature Conservancy Council and other interested bodies about these recommendations. As a result there followed discussions between the Department of Agriculture and Fisheries for Scotland and the Nature Conservancy Council culminating in the appointment of a Working Party.

Under the Chairmanship of Professor C. H. Gimingham of the Botany Department at the University of Aberdeen this Working Party* addressed itself to the following tasks which comprised its remit:

(i) to evaluate existing knowledge and to note any need for further research, and

(ii) to produce a draft of a *Guide to Good Muirburn Practice* for discussion.

This booklet is the result of the second of these and is primarily intended for use by land owners, managers and tenants who are the practitioners responsible for muirburn. It is hoped that the Guide will also provide a concise theoretical and practical basis for students and advisers who may wish to study the management practice of muirburn in more detail.

*Members of the Working Party are listed in Appendix No. 1.

1

Note: Much of what is contained in this Guide will be applicable outside Scotland but it should be noted that the burning of heather and grass in England and Wales is controlled under the provisions of Section 20 of the Hill Farming Act 1946 and the following regulations made under that Section:

Statutory Instrument 1949 No. 386:	*The Heather and Grass Burning (England and Wales) Regulations, 1949*
Statutory Instrument 1958 No. 4:	*The Heather and Grass Burning (Northumberland and Durham) Regulations, 1958.*
and Statutory Instrument 1975 No. 112:	*The Heather and Grass Burning (Amendment) (Northumberland and Durham) Regulations, 1975.*

ACKNOWLEDGEMENTS

The Working Party acknowledge invaluable information given so freely by many landowners, farmers, managers, keepers and interested organisations. Special thanks are due to Mr. E. L. Birse and Mr. J. Bibby of the Macaulay Institute for Soil Research who provided useful advice on aspects of the vegetation map and to the clerical and cartographic staff of the Department of Agriculture and Fisheries for Scotland and Nature Conservancy Council for their services in collation, drafting and typing.

Department of Agriculture and Fisheries for Scotland
Nature Conservancy Council

A Guide to Good Muirburn Practice

MUIRBURN WORKING PARTY

Edinburgh   Her Majesty's Stationery Office

ISBN 0 11 491463 X

II

Introduction

Muirburn is a means of managing the vegetation of upland grazings and grouse moors to maintain it in a productive condition. Periodic burning prevents invasion by trees and shrubs, but its main objective is to clear away aging herbage when this declines in feeding-value, productivity and accessibility to grazing animals, as dead or woody material accumulates. Properly carried out, muirburn is followed by a rapid regeneration of forage plants, providing a new supply of young, nutritious shoots and minimising the risk of spread of unwanted species. Burning may also be used to clear the ground in preparation for tree planting or colonization, as a preliminary to reseeding with grasses, and in making fire-breaks.

The use of fire in the management of upland grazings has a long history. Ever since the forest, which formerly covered much of Scotland, was cleared, muirburn has been used at intervals for the purposes outlined above. Where productivity was relatively low and the terrain rough, a cheap but effective means of management was required, capable of controlling large areas with minimum demands on man-power.

With the advent of large-scale hill sheep farming, it became necessary to burn the vegetation on a regular basis. This is because, owing to limitations imposed by winter keep, the stocking rates on hill grazings are low and as a result utilization of the yearly production of herbage in the summer season is also low. Hence there is an excess of production over utilization. Where heather is the chief plant grazed, this excess production is channelled into the growth of woody stems and branches. In hill grasslands the unused leaves and flowering culms die and accumulate in the pasture. In both cases burning removes these accumulations and restores the communities to a condition of fresh young growth which is more attractive, accessible and nutritious to grazing animals.

3

In addition to its use in the management of hill grazings for sheep and cattle, muirburn is also an essential part of grouse-moor management. Here, because grouse depend very largely on heather for food, the purpose of muirburn is to maintain the dominance of heather and prevent it becoming leggy. By regular burning in small strips or patches, some of the heather is kept short to promote maximum production of green, edible shoots per unit area, while nearby older patches offer shelter and cover.

Different types of vegetation require burning at differing frequencies and the choice of an appropriate burning cycle can make the difference between good and bad management. Some types should not be burned at all. Fire has considerable effects upon the vegetation and its habitat, and upon the native wild plants, animals and birds of the uplands. Even when care is exercised there is always a danger of damage to neighbouring property or plantations; while irresponsible or uncontrolled burning may cause lasting damage to the areas being burned. Observance of the provisions contained in legislation (which makes muirburn legal only between certain dates) is a first step in avoiding unnecessary damage to property, wildlife and game.

Causes for concern

Properly used, in those parts of the country and on those vegetation types for which it is appropriate, muirburn is an important management tool which will achieve its objectives with a minimum of undesirable effects. There are, however, numerous instances of the mis-use of muirburn. It is, for example, sometimes employed where climate or vegetation are unsuitable, or under inappropriate weather conditions. A lack of planning may result in a given area being burnt over too frequently. Indiscriminate or uncontrolled burning may give rise to fires which become excessively hot or spread over too great an area. In all these cases, regeneration of the vegetation may be delayed, unwanted plants may invade, erosion may set in, and wild life as well as domestic stock may suffer.

It is all too easy to employ fire without sufficient consideration of its ultimate effects. For this reason, the suggestions contained in this Guide are offered in the hope that the rules it sets out for good muirburn practice will seem reasonable, and will be widely adopted.

III
The Legal Position

The making of muirburn in Scotland is subject to the provisions of the Hill Farming Act, 1946, of which the relevant sections are quoted in Appendix 2. The Act states that "making muirburn" includes setting fire to or burning any heath or muir. In practice, "heath or muir" has been held to include not only ground on which heather grows but all moors or uplands, whatever may be growing on them.

This Guide is concerned with muirburn as practised by landowners or tenants of land for the purpose of maintaining or improving the production from that land. It is not therefore concerned with legal problems relating to fires caused by unauthorised persons, whether deliberately or accidentally. These apart, the main provisions of the Act are:

(1) Muirburn is lawful only from 1st October to 15th April inclusive. (An extension of this period to 30th April, or on land over 1500 feet above sea level to 15th May, is legal for the proprietor of any lands, or for tenants if they have written authority from the proprietor. The Secretary of State may also extend the period, within the above limits, for any lands in any year).

(2) The Act confers on a tenant the right to make muirburn, but that tenant must under Section 24 give 28 days' notice in writing to the proprietor of his intention to make muirburn. If the proprietor is dissatisfied as to the location or extent of the proposed burning, he must inform his tenant within 7 days and then refer the matter to the Secretary of State for decision.

(3) It is an offence:
   (i) To commence to make muirburn between one hour after sunset and one hour before sunrise.

5

(ii) To fail to provide sufficient staff and equipment to control burning operations so as to prevent damage to woodlands or any adjoining lands, march fences, or other subjects.

(iii) For any person to fail to give the adjoining proprietors of lands and woodlands not less than 24 hours' notice in writing of his intention to make muirburn.

(iv) For a tenant to fail to give his proprietor similar warning (in addition to the prior 28 days' written notice as set out in (2) above).

(v) To make muirburn on any land without due care so as to cause damage to any woodlands, adjoining lands, march fences or other subjects.

In certain circumstances muirburn may be affected by other Acts of Parliament. Under the Clean Air Act (1956), Section 16, the production of smoke may be forbidden if it becomes "a nuisance to the inhabitants of a neighbourhood". Where Tree Preservation Orders have been imposed under the Town and Country Planning (Scotland) Act 1972 and earlier legislation, designated trees and woods are protected against damage.

The need to conform to these provisions is stressed as an essential part of good muirburn practice. However, as the following Sections indicate, good practice requires not only observance of the law, but careful attention to a variety of important factors.

IV

Plant Names

Popular names of plants vary from one locality to another. To avoid confusion, a list is given below of those plants which receive frequent mention in the following pages, showing (i) the name adopted in this Guide, (ii) the scientific name, (iii) some commonly-used alternative English names and (iv) some Gaelic equivalents. There are, in addition, many names of more restricted local occurrence which it would be impossible to include. This is particularly the case of Gaelic names.

(i) Name Used in the Guide	(ii) Scientific name	(iii) Alternative English names	(iv) Some Gaelic equivalents
Bell heather	*Erica cinerea*	Heath	Fraoch a' bhadain
Bent grasses:	*Agrostis* species:		
Common bent	*Agrostis tenuis*		Fioran, Fior-than
Brown bent	*Agrostis canina*	Brown top	Muran cuartach
Blaeberry	*Vaccinium myrtillus*	Bilberry, Whortleberry	Lus nan dearc, Corra-mheagan, Gear-dhearc
Bog moss	*Sphagnum* species		Mointeach liath, Fionnlach
Bracken	*Pteridium aquilinum*		Raineach mhòr
Cloudberry	*Rubus chamaemorus*		Oighreag, oireag
Cotton sedge	*Eriophorum* species:		
	Eriophorum angustifolium	Greater Cotton-grass Common Cotton-grass	Canach, Bàrr fhionn
	Eriophorum vaginatum	Lesser Cotton-grass Draw-moss, Hare's tail, Mossine	Sioda monaidh

7

(i) Name Used in the Guide	(ii) Scientific name	(iii) Alternative English names	(iv) Some Gaelic equivalents
Cross-leaved heath	*Erica tetralix*	Bog heather	Fraoch frangach, Fraoch an ruinnse
Crowberry	*Empetrum nigrum*		Lus na fionnaig
Deer sedge	*Trichophorum cespitosum*	Deer grass	Ciob cheann dubh, Cruach luachair
Fescue grasses: Sheep's fescue Red fescue	*Festuca* species: *Festuca ovina* *Festuca rubra*	Creeping fescue	Feur-chaorach
Flying bent	*Molinia caerulea*	Purple moor grass, Blow-grass, White grass*	Bunglàs, Punglàs, Braban
Heather	*Calluna vulgaris*	Ling	Fraoch, Langa
Heath rush	*Juncus squarrosus*	Stool bent	Bru-corcur, Bru-chorachd
Mat-grass	*Nardus stricta*	White bent, White grass*	Beitein, Eanach fionnach
Scottish cranberry	*Vaccinium vitis-idaea*	Cowberry	Braoileag, Lus nam broighleag
Sweet Vernal Grass	*Anthoxanthum odoratum*		Mislean, Borrach
Wavy hair-grass	*Deschampsia flexuosa*		Mion fheur
Whin	*Ulex europaeus*	Gorse	Conasg

* The name "white grass", commonly applied (particularly in south Scotland) to *Nardus stricta*, is also used for *Molinia caerulea* especially in the north.

V

Climate, Soils and Vegetation

At the present time muirburn is carried on, throughout Scotland, on a variety of vegetation types and under a considerable range of climatic conditions. Since it will be necessary in later Chapters of this Guide to make separate reference to these, the following scheme provides a broad series of categories most of which are subject to management by burning, although to varying extents.

A generalised map of the principal vegetation types within the three climatic areas of Scotland appears on the centre pages.

A. NORTHERN CLIMATIC AREA

Cool summers, winter temperatures not severe, but liable to severe gales; rainfall variable.

Soil Type	Vegetation Type
1. Acid soils with peaty humus at surface and thin iron pan in subsoil (peaty podzols).	(a) Northern heather moor—often with crowberry.
	(b) Moist heather moor—some cross-leaved heath, flying bent and deer sedge.
2. Poorly drained soils with surface peat (peaty gleys) and shallow blanket peat.	(a) Moist heather moor (as above).
	(b) Wet Moor with cross-leaved heath—frequent burning may give rise to deer sedge moor.
3. Blanket peat—merging to upland blanket peat (hill peat).	(a) Blanket bog and upland blanket bog—mixtures of cotton sedge, deer sedge, flying bent and heather, with abundant bog moss.

B. EASTERN CLIMATIC AREA

Warmer summers and colder winters; low to medium rainfall (e.g. 750–1300 mm; 30–50 in.)

Soil Type	*Vegetation Type*
1. Freely drained brown soils.	(a) Bent-fescue grassland with bracken—local.
	(b) Heather moor with variety of flowering plants and grasses.
	(c) Whin scrub.
2. Freely drained acid soils with surface raw humus (podzols).	(a) Dry northern heather moor, often with blaeberry, Scottish cranberry and crowberry.
	(b) Whin scrub.
3. Imperfectly drained acid soils with peaty humus at surface and thin iron pan (peaty podzols).	(a) Moist heather moor—some cross-leaved heath, flying bent and deer sedge.
	(b) Wet moor with cross-leaved heath (local).
4. Imperfectly drained humic brown soils, or peaty podzols—mainly south of River Tay.	(a) Mat-grass.
	(b) Flying bent grassland.
5. Upland blanket peat (hill peat).	(a) Upland blanket bog with heather, cotton sedge and cloudberry.

C. WESTERN CLIMATIC AREA

Rather cool summers and mild winters; high rainfall (over 1500 mm; 50 in.)

Soil Type	*Vegetation Type*
1. Freely drained brown soils.	(a) Bent-fescue grassland with bracken.
	(b) Heather moor with variety of flowering plants and grasses.
2. Freely drained acid soils with surface raw humus (podzols) and some peaty podzols.	(a) Dry western heather moor.
	(b) Moist heather moor.
3. Imperfectly drained humic brown soils.	(a) Mat-grass.
4. Peaty soils (podzols and gleys) and shallow peat.	(a) Moist heather moor with cross-leaved heath, flying bent and deer sedge.
	(b) Flying bent grassland.
	(c) Mat-grass.

Soil Type	Vegetation Type
5. Shallow blanket peat.	(a) Wet moor with cross-leaved heath, often with abundant flying bent.
6. Blanket peat.	(a) Blanket bog with flying bent and (often) sweet gale (*Myrica gale*).
7. Upland blanket peat (hill peat).	(a) Upland blanket bog.

VI

Plant Response to Fire

The most common dominants of regularly burnt ground are heather, flying
bent, bracken, deer sedge, mat-grass, cotton sedge, heath rush and cross-
leaved heath. Heather and flying bent, either singly or together, occupy vast
areas of rangeland throughout the Highlands; while on well-drained ground,
particularly in south and west Scotland, bracken may be predominant
almost to the complete exclusion of other herbage. Of these plants, only
heather is completely evergreen and grazed throughout the year. The fresh
young growth of flying bent is grazed from spring to summer, while deer
sedge is of more limited use, from late spring to summer. After this their
shoots become fibrous and unpalatable before dying back in autumn. Cotton
sedge is valuable especially in early Spring, though it is grazed at other times
of the year as well. Mat-grass has little value, and bracken is quite worthless
except as bedding and shelter.

These plants are not all equally resistant to fire and it is possible to cause
the replacement of one with another by repeated burning, especially when
coupled with heavy grazing. Such replacement may not readily be reversed,
for example, in the case of replacement of heather by bracken. Differences
amongst species in their tolerance of fire depend on their growth form and
means of reproduction.

Heather

Heather is a low shrub, seldom exceeding 1 m (approx. 3 feet) in height. It
branches repeatedly from near the base and can form dense stands that
suppress almost all other plants. Reproduction is largely by means of seed,
but after burning, heather also has the capacity to regenerate vegetatively by
sprouting from buds situated close to the ground on the stem-bases left

behind by the fire. Although large numbers of the small, light seeds are produced each year, seedling establishment is generally erratic and initial growth slow. On the other hand, shoots developing from surviving stem bases have the advantage of a fully developed root system with stored food reserves. By this means, total cover may be restored within 3 or 4 years after burning, much faster than from seedlings alone. The dense growth habit, the production of enormous quantities of viable seed, and the ability to regenerate fairly rapidly after fire make it easy to understand why heather is such a successful plant in a habitat managed almost exclusively by burning.

However, heather is by no means invulnerable to fire. In the first place, with increasing age there are fewer individual stems in a stand of heather, and their capacity to sprout from the base declines. Secondly, severe burning can destroy the buds from which the clusters of new shoots arise.

Fire temperature is influenced by weather and other conditions (Chapter VII), but the older the stand, the greater are the chances of an excessively hot fire and therefore the lower the chances of good vegetative regeneration. This is clearly undesirable, and hot fires in old heather are singularly unproductive (Photos 4 and 5). Whereas moderate fires in heather stands aged between about 7 and 15 years permit vegetative regeneration and gentle heating may actually improve seed germination, very hot fires in old heather destroy the plants completely. Regeneration is then from seed alone, which being slow, provides opportunities for unwanted fire-resistant plants to invade and spread over the ground. At the extreme, even buried seeds may be charred by combustion of the surface humus, or the fire may leave an unsuitable seed bed, and then the regeneration of heather may fail completely.

Grasses, sedges and rushes

In contrast to heather, the tussocky growth habit of flying bent is supremely well adapted to withstand burning. The buds that produce new tillers are normally quite unaffected by fire because they are buried some 5 cm (2 in.) or more below the outer surface of the tussock. Only a severe fire when the peat catches alight is likely to damage them. More or less the same is true of the other tussocky plants of hill grazings, such as cotton sedge and, to a lesser extent, mat-grass and heath rush. Moreover, all these species produce abundant seed that germinates readily and are therefore well able to exploit new niches created by burning.

Bracken

The deeply buried rhizome of bracken similarly confers on the plant a degree of immunity to fire. Although bracken seems to establish only rarely from the abundant spores produced each year, the rhizome enables it to spread rapidly and vigorously into vacant ground. New bracken fronds emerge in May and June—too late to be damaged by spring burning. It is difficult to know whether the spread of bracken over the past 50–150 years is the result of bad burning management, climatic trends, changes in the cattle/sheep stocking ratios or the cessation of the practice of cutting bracken for bedding. Probably all have played their part.

All these plants will reappear after burning, but their particular characteristics, some of which have been mentioned above, determine the rate of recovery. This varies considerably: heather, for example, is slower to recover than flying bent or deer sedge. It follows that when some of these plants are present together in mixture, burning will give an advantage to whichever can recover most quickly. In this way, repeated burning of a mixture of heather and flying bent may lead to the virtual disappearance of heather and its replacement by the flying bent. For the same reason, some plants such as blaeberry or sweet vernal grass are almost always reduced in amount or even eliminated by systematic burning.

VII
Action of Fire

The success of muirburn depends largely on the amount of heat generated. In some fires, the temperatures reached are sufficient only to scorch the vegetation, leaving large amounts of debris. On the other hand, a really severe fire may burn off not only the vegetation but also any surface layer of peaty humus. Often this is the outcome of fires that creep slowly over ground, exposing it to prolonged heating. Thus the "intensity" of a fire is governed, not only by the heat of the flames, but also by the rate at which they spread. Good practice demands a fire of medium "intensity", mid-way between the extremes outlined above—both of which amount to bad practice.

Temperatures in muirburn

Fires commonly travel at rates of 2 to 7 m (2–8 yards) per minute, but these can be greatly exceeded under certain weather conditions. In heather, they produce high temperatures among the foliage and branches of the bushes (500°–800°C or even more) but it is much cooler at ground level. Here the maximum temperatures are usually 250°–500°C, and these seldom last for more than one minute, followed by rapid cooling. The degree and duration of heating in grass fires have not been measured in Scotland.

Where, however, the surface peat or humus is set alight the consequences may be extremely serious. Such fires are difficult to extinguish and may smoulder for days on end, eventually burning down to the underlying mineral material, exposing rocks and boulders. A fire of such severity should be avoided at all costs because recovery of the vegetation will certainly be long-delayed.

15

Controlling the intensity of muirburn

An experienced man is well able to regulate the intensity of a fire within broad limits. The correct conditions for burning can be identified by taking account of the various factors that affect fire intensity.

(a) *Weather*. This is perhaps the most important consideration. In most years there is a spell of warm sunny weather in March or April. Burning in these dry conditions demands great care because a low atmospheric humidity coupled with a moderate wind that fans the flames can produce an especially fierce fire. At the other extreme, it is difficult to start a fire on damp windless days and the result is often unsatisfactory because large amounts of unburnt material are left behind. On dry, windless days, it is also particularly difficult to control fires. Equally, it is useless to try to burn tall thick-stemmed heather in a strong wind: apart from the danger of losing control, the flames run only through the crowns of the plants and leave the long woody stems unburnt. The usual rule is to burn only in a gentle breeze.

(b) *Vegetation*. The amount of plant material available to be burned, its composition and moisture content are all important. In heather, the older stands usually give rise to hotter fires than younger ones because there is more to burn, and a bigger proportion consists of wood. The vegetation as a whole contains less moisture, and this aids combustion. Where there is an intimate mixture of plant material and oxygen more heat is produced. For this reason, finely branched heather or a loosely packed accumulation of dead flying bent can burn rapidly with great heat, but densely packed damp vegetation will not burn at all.

(c) *Soil surface*. Both the type of soil and its moisture content affect the temperatures at and immediately below ground level. For example, the surface of a wet peat is less readily heated than that of a dry mineral soil. Litter, mosses and lichens all insulate against heat, but with varying degrees of efficiency. Dense carpets or cushions of water-retentive mosses are excellent insulators, except in very dry conditions, but heather litter and loose mats of dry mosses or lichens are less good.

(d) *Burning technique*. The normal practice is to let the fire run with the wind. Results vary according to the interplay of the factors mentioned above. However, where the vegetation is particularly luxuriant or otherwise difficult to burn by the conventional method, it is sometimes "back-burnt", i.e. burnt against the wind. Back-burning produces a very slow-moving fire which exposes the ground to prolonged heating. This can have undesirable results if used in the wrong circumstances, but may be useful, for example, for burning old heather on wet boggy ground or on damp north-facing slopes. The technique is also valuable in creating limited areas of clean ground which act as fire-breaks.

Consequences of burning at the wrong temperature

The immediately obvious effects of fires that are either too hot or not hot enough have already been mentioned. However there are other harmful consequences of burning at the wrong temperature.

(a) *Excessively hot fires.* The top 10–15 cm (4–6 in.) of peaty humus on hill soils contains a mass of plant roots, vegetative buds and buried seed as well as a myriad of small organisms. Any serious charring of this zone, or the complete exposure of mineral soil, effectively sterilises the ground. Regeneration of the higher plants is long-delayed, only mosses and lichens can colonise readily, and the soil becomes liable to erosion. Wherever bare rock or scree is exposed, regeneration may never occur. Thus severe burning can be a prescription for the creation of barren areas.

Very hot fires may involve a risk of depleting the stock of plant nutrients. Even in normal fires, in which temperatures do not exceed 500°C the smoke carries away a substantial amount of the carbon, sulphur and nitrogen which was contained in the vegetation. These losses are increased by prolonged or severe heating, when the smoke may also incorporate significant amounts of potassium, magnesium, calcium and phosphorus.

These mineral nutrients are also present in the ash deposited on the ground during a fire. Some of them may be dissolved in rainwater, but if this drains through a layer of organic matter at the soil surface the nutrients may be retained there to some extent. However should a very hot fire have destroyed this layer, these nutrients may be lost as the water drains away or runs off the surface. Although the effects of fire on the "fund" of plant nutrients are by no means fully understood as yet, a considerable amount of research work has been devoted to this topic.

With normal, well-controlled burning, the losses of nutrients in smoke and by solution in rainwater may not, in most cases, exceed their accumulation from various sources (particularly rainfall and, in coastal districts, fine sprays) in the period between successive fires. This is illustrated by Fig. 1 which also shows that where the land is used for sheep production, additional losses resulting from the sale of live-stock are not normally large enough to make a substantial difference. Phosphorus, however, may constitute an exception to these conclusions, for the amounts contributed in rainfall are generally small.

17

Fig. 1. Diagram illustrating the main sources of Nutrient Input and Loss in Vegetation Subject to Burning and Grazing.

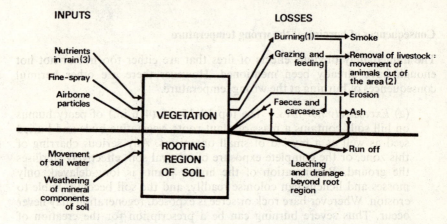

Some Examples of Quantities Involved (Figures in kilograms per hectare per year)

	Nitrogen	Phosphorus	Calcium	Potassium
(1) Losses due to Burning Heather Moorland (average per year if burnt once in 10 years)	4–6	0·3–0·6	0·2–0·4	0·5–0·8
(2) Losses Due to Sale of Ewes and Lambs*				
i) Stocking Rate 1·5–2 ha/ewe (4–5 acres/ewe); Less than 70% Lambing; Liveweight sold 10 kg/ha (9 lbs/acre)	0·3	0·05	0·09	0·016
ii) 0·5–1 ha/ewe (1–2 acres/ewe); 70% Lambing; Liveweight Sold 40 kg/ha (36 lbs/acre)	1·2	0·20	0·36	0·064
iii) 0·5–1 ha/ewe; over 100% Lambing; Liveweight Sold 80 kg/ha (72 lbs/acre)	2·4	0·40	0·72	0·128
(3) Inputs in Rainfall				
i) Kerloch, Nr. Banchory, Kincardineshire	8·9	0·2	6·7	3·9
ii) Leanachan, West Inverness-shire	14·8	0·44	7·2	13·3

Figures are available for only a few of the sources of input and loss. However, they serve to show that except for phosphorus, the combined losses per year due to burning and sale of sheep do not exceed inputs in rainfall, although the latter are not necessarily retained completely in the soil. It is possible that slow depletion of phosphorus may be taking place.

* *Footnote:* Body composition figures of 3·0% N, 0·5% P, 0·89% Ca, 0·16% K, were used, based on grams/kilogram liveweight as published by the Agriculture Research Council in their Technical Review of 1965 on *The Nutrient Requirement of Farm Livestock No. 2—Ruminants.*

It must, however, be emphasized that there are very strong reasons for avoiding excessively hot fires, which may lead to serious depletion of the nutrient "fund".

(b) *Fires which are not hot enough.* Fires that consume less than half of the vegetation to be burned must be considered unsatisfactory on two counts. Firstly, the mass of unburnt vegetation, usually with a layer of undisturbed mosses and litter, slows the growth of new vegetation shoots by shading and obstruction; moreover, grazing animals may be denied easy access to any shoots that do penetrate the debris. Secondly, an unburnt carpet of loosely packed moss, lichens or litter is liable to dry out readily, slowing the rate of seedling establishment. In this way fires which are not hot enough can also impede the rapid regeneration of heather and other plants. However, such fires are not so likely to be as disastrous as those which are excessively hot.

VIII

Guidelines for Muirburn

Fire as a management technique

The main problems lie in deciding how frequently vegetation should be burned and how much of a grazing or grouse moor should be burned at any one time.

Burning should be carried out according to a planned management programme. This is particularly important where labour is scarce, and in areas where suitable weather conditions are of infrequent occurrence. Lack of a plan often results in neglect of north-facing slopes because occasions when these are dry enough to burn may be infrequent, whereas there is a temptation to overburn those which face to the south and dry out more rapidly. The overall plan for a grazing should take account of the vegetational make-up of that area. The various vegetation types contribute to production in different ways and at different times of year. Their reaction to burning also varies, and it is of the first importance to have a clear view of the objectives on any grazing. Burning to a plan requires that areas in need of burning should be carefully noted, together with other factors such as the wind direction appropriate to the burning of a particular area and whether a fire-break exists, e.g. a stream or a recently burned vegetation patch. In the absence of a fire-break, conditions which are rather too damp for ideal burning may offer the opportunity to create one, thus enabling practice to approach the plan more closely. Burning which is left until very late in the season, or where control is inadequate, means that unduly large areas get burnt, creating both utilization and management problems for the future.

Weather conditions are sometimes suitable for burning in autumn and, whenever possible this practice is to be encouraged. Contrary to some opinions, there is evidence that results may be as good as, or in regard to heather regeneration even better than, with spring fires. Moreover, if some

1. Starting the fire. The heather is ignited with a paraffin lighter at intervals along the starting line. A wire beater for controlling the fire edge is also shown.

Photo: D. A. Gowans.

Photo: *C. H. Gimingham.*

2. Controlling the margins of the fire, using scrapers.

3. Good heather burning producing a mosaic of patches of varying age.

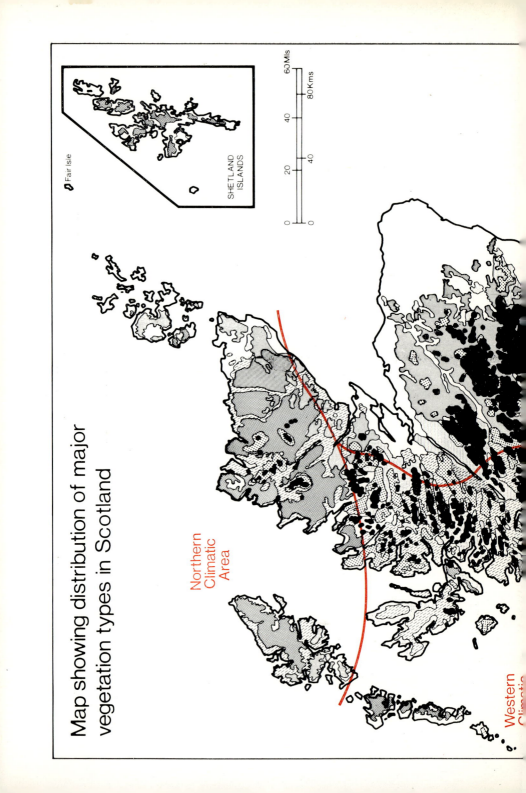

Map showing distribution of major vegetation types in Scotland

Fair Isle

SHETLAND ISLANDS

60Mls
80Kms

Northern Climatic Area

Western Climatic

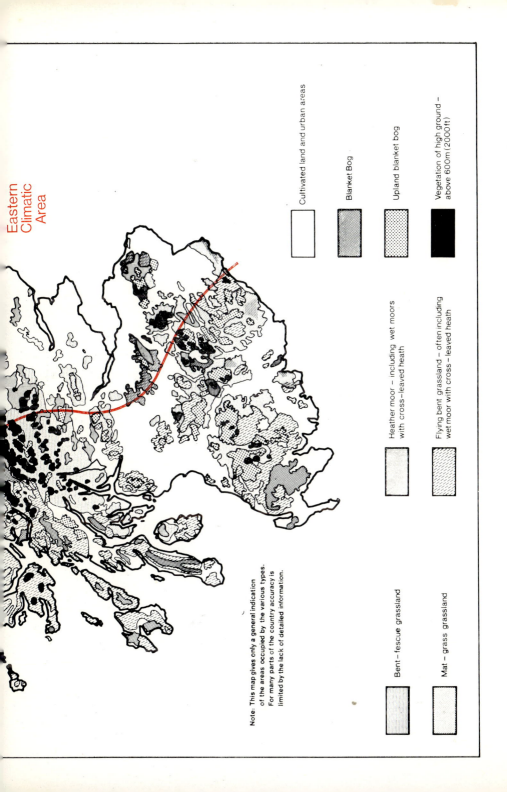

Eastern Climatic Area

Note: This map gives only a general indication of the areas occupied by the various types. For many parts of the country accuracy is limited by the lack of detailed information.

Cultivated land and urban areas

Blanket Bog

Upland blanket bog

Vegetation of high ground – above 600m (2000ft)

Heather moor – including wet moors with cross-leaved heath

Flying bent grassland – often including wet moor with cross-leaved heath

Bent-fescue grassland

Mat-grass grassland

4. Heather burning in long narrow strips suitable for grouse-moor management.
    (The stand in the foreground has been allowed to get too old before burning. Lengths of
    stem are left behind and regeneration is poor).

Photo: G. R. Miller.

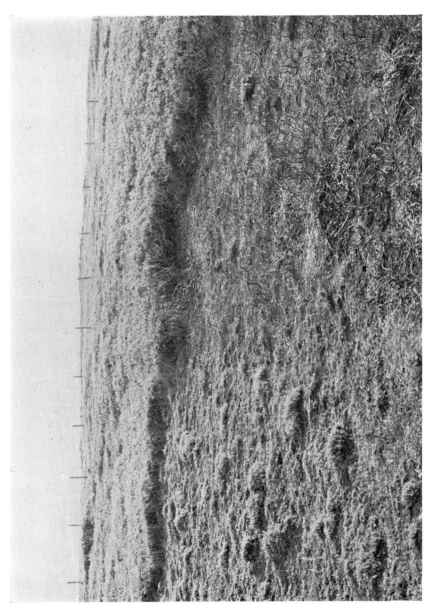

5. Good regeneration (left) after burning heather at the correct stage, alongside poor regeneration (right) where the stand was too old before burning. The condition of the stands before burning may be judged from the unburnt heather beyond. Photo taken 18 months after burning. *Photo: G. R. Miller.*

6. Scree formation due to burning steep slopes at 500 m in eastern Scotland.

burning is achieved in autumn the chances of failure to complete the programme by mid-April of the following year because of bad weather are correspondingly reduced.

Management of vegetation dominated by heather

(i) *Identification of stand condition for burning*

Heather grows at different rates depending on soil type, aspect, altitude, exposure and grazing pressure. Hence, decisions about when to burn should be determined by stand condition rather than age. The most useful single indicator of stand condition is the height of the heather.

Where heather occurs in pure stands, with few other plants, there is often sufficient plant material available for a good clean burn by the time it has reached about 20 cm (8 in.), and as a general rule most of the heather should be burned before it becomes as tall as 30 cm (12 in.). Burning at this stage on peaty soils should result in rapid regeneration, though on hard ground, at high altitudes and in very wet conditions regrowth will be slower (photo 5). However, it is usually desirable to treat some patches differently and allow them to grow on to about 40 cm (16 in.) to offer cover for grouse or winter feed in snow for stock or deer.

Where heather grows in mixture with grasses, the usual objective is to maintain heather dominance and burning should be delayed until the plants are a little taller and the accompanying grasses weakened by shading. However, on hills where the grasses are bents and fescues, a farmer may be happy for the proportion of these to increase. This can be encouraged by a judicious combination of burning and grazing. He will be less happy if flying bent or mat-grass increase. The former sheds its leaves each autumn and provides no winter grazing while the latter has but poor feeding value and is no improvement on heather.

Where heather is mixed with flying bent, particularly in the wetter areas of the west, account must be taken of the range of vegetation types available on a grazing. Heather, though of value as a winter feed, is of too poor a quality on its own for ewes with lambs in late spring and early summer. If there are no bent-fescue patches or other green ground available, it will be necessary to burn a proportion of the hill according to the shorter rotation appropriate for flying bent so that the fresh growth of this grass will provide some grazing during early summer (for details see p. 25). The remainder of the grazing should be burned on a longer rotation so that plants such as heather and cotton sedge are encouraged. Deer sedge, like flying bent, only provides grazing during spring and summer. Where it is mixed with heather and flying bent, management should follow the lines suggested for the mixture of heather and flying bent.

21

Bracken tends to invade heather wherever the soil conditions are suitable. While too frequent burning may well hasten this invasion, it is doubtful whether the most careful burning management, or even absence of burning, could halt the spread of bracken. The most that can be said is that it may be desirable to let heather grow tall and dense enough to offer some competition to the bracken before burning. However it should not be allowed to become too aged as this would result in slower regeneration which, like too frequent burning, could favour the spread of bracken.

Although, as stated above, the usual objective of heather management is to maintain its dominance and productivity, where extensive stands occur under conditions of climate and soil suitable for bent-fescue pastures, it may be desirable to replace some of the heather by grassland. Burning may be a first step in this process, with extra heavy grazing during the regeneration phase to reduce the vigour of the young heather in relation to that of the grasses. Such a change in botanical composition of the grazing is further encouraged by additions of lime and fertilizer.

(ii) *The proportion of a heather moor to be burned and size of individual fires*
The proportion to be burned in any year will be determined largely by the average time taken for the heather to reach the appropriate condition for burning, e.g. if the regrowth period is eight years the aim should be one-eighth, if fifteen years one-fifteenth, and so on. The size and shape of individual fires will depend upon whether the moor is being burned for grouse, sheep or deer. For grouse the fire shape is as important as size. Long narrow strips up to thirty metres wide are preferable so that the protective cover of taller heather is never too far away (Photos 3 and 4). For sheep, the fires should be much smaller than the rake of a heft of sheep so that more than one age of heather is provided within their grazing area. Ideally, a patch mosaic of various ages of heather would be the aim as this would aid the distribution of stock over the whole grazing. Deer have a much larger grazing rake than sheep and a great part of the land they graze, especially in summer, is not normally burned because of its altitude and the nature of the terrain. In general, however, burning for deer will probably best be served by following practices similar to those advocated for sheep.

In deciding on the size of the individual fires, inevitably a compromise must be reached between the ideal of many small fires and the limitations due to the nature of the terrain, shortage of labour to control the fires, suitable weather conditions and the need to burn an adequate proportion of the grazing in any one year. These difficulties should not however be made an excuse for abandoning any attempt at a planned burning programme.

(iii) *Maintaining healthy heather*
Disease and damage of heather are usually shown up by a change of colour. The foliage first becomes a dull green, then brown and finally, when dead, grey or almost silvery. These changes may be due to one of several causes:—

22

(a) "Winter-browning". This is widespread every year at high altitudes but is less frequent, though sometimes extensive, on low ground. It may occur in any month from December to April, though most commonly in January and February, when the green shoots turn reddish brown at first, then becoming dull brown or grey. Because it is frequently associated with frosty weather, the term "frosting" has been applied, but the effect is probably caused by desiccation, usually when the soil is frozen and not thickly covered by snow. Although the amount of edible material available may be severely reduced, the plants are not normally killed and regrowth will take place in the following summer. No special measures are needed to promote recovery.

(b) Heather beetle (*Lochmaea suturalis*). An attacked plant often has a fox-red colour, but this is not necessarily indicative of beetle damage, since it may result from other causes including drought, frost, scorching at the margin of a fire, or other unfavourable conditions. Plants damaged by heather beetle can be recognised by the development of the red colouration in late summer and by the loss of many leaves and much of the bark of the finer shoots by the gnawing of the insects. Severe attacks may decimate extensive areas, but outbreaks are usually patchy and local, though worst on rather flat marshy ground.

The beetle grubs feed on heather shoots in July and August, later leaving the plant and pupating in the surface litter below. Adult beetles emerge in August and September and return to feed on the heather shoots. Some of these hibernate below the plants until the following April when egg laying takes place. Unfortunately, the burning season is over before beetles and grubs are to be found on the plants, so they cannot be directly controlled by muirburn. Furthermore, by the time infestation is noticeable many of the beetles may have moved to surrounding areas, so there would be more chance of killing them by burning adjoining stands rather than those which have been most severely damaged.

However, the best method of reducing (though not eliminating) beetle damage is probably by consistently good management of the heather moors over a long period of time, and the occurrence of beetle outbreaks should not become an excuse for burning abnormally large areas. There is evidence to suggest that damage is worst where heather is not maintained in a vigorous and productive condition.

(c) Heather rhizomorph fungus (or "horsehair fungus", *Marasmius androsaceus*). This fungus occurs frequently in wet or poorly drained habitats, where damp moss (particularly bog moss) surrounds the base of the plants. Its effects are more severe on old heather, especially when long woody stems have developed. The presence of the fungus may be confirmed by finding the hair-like "rhizomorphs" which pass

23

from stem to stem near the base of the plants, or the small "toadstools" on thin stalks which appear on the older parts of the stems. The production of green shoots is greatly reduced and infected plants turn first brown, then grey, creating a conspicuous patch as the twigs die back. In the north and west of Scotland, where conditions are wet and the weather makes regular burning difficult, quite extensive areas of heather may be affected, but new growth may follow after a good clean burn. Production of young heather is less affected, and again it seems that the best long-term protection is afforded by a well-planned burning policy which keeps the heather relatively short and densely branched, at the same time reducing the moss cover around the stem bases. Under certain circumstances, improved drainage may also assist in control.

(iv) *Drainage*

Heather is most productive on freely-drained soils. In the wetter, western climatic area and wherever soils are badly drained, improvement of drainage may contribute to the maintenance of healthy stands of heather, and provide a useful back-up to good muirburn practice. (Mole or tine draining may be employed where appropriate).

However, in view of the high costs of drainage it is important to bear in mind that the benefits are greatest on the shallow peats and mineral soils, whereas on deeper peats and blanket bog much of the improvement is restricted to the margins of the drains.

Management of vegetation dominated by grasses

The burning of grassy moors is still widely practised where flying bent is dominant and more occasionally on mat-grass areas. Low utilization by stock leads to the accumulation of dead grass leaves within two to four years so that the earliness and accessibility of fresh growth is reduced. Thus burning rotations are usually short, with three years being the average.

Flying bent on eastern, drier grassy moors usually occurs along with other grasses such as wavy hair grass, sheep's fescue and brown bent. Unlike flying bent, these grasses provide some grazing over winter. They are less fire resistant, but better able to stand up to grazing. In these areas, if fires are large so that the regrowth is poorly grazed, muirburn becomes self-defeating as it leads to an increasing dominance of flying bent. The proportion of the grazing burnt should be small enough therefore to ensure that the burned areas are subsequently well grazed. Fires should be well distributed in an attempt to avoid large unbroken tracts of unburnt vegetation which make fire control another day very difficult. (A moor may first be divided up by a number of long narrow fires, or by burning fire-breaks, to facilitate later burning of smaller strips or patches). High grazing pressures, as well as encouraging a more mixed species composition, would delay the accumulation of uneaten herbage and hence lessen the need for further burning. Under more intensive systems of sheep farming in grass moor areas the increased grazing pressure may eliminate the need to burn.

On western moors flying bent and heather are often found growing in association. The problem is whether burning management should be according to the longer heather rotation or the shorter flying bent rotation. Burning mixed heather and flying bent on a short rotation will favour flying bent at the expense of the heather. Heather is an important source of winter feed for both sheep and deer. Flying bent only assumes importance as early summer feed on grazings where patches of bent-fescue or green hill are absent. Where this is the case a certain proportion of the land should be burned on a short rotation. No more land should be burned than is necessary to provide sufficient fresh accessible growth to support the stock carried. To achieve this it will often be necessary to burn fire-breaks in less than ideal conditions. The reasons for avoiding overlarge fires are to reduce the area on which too frequent burning can lead to the elimination of heather, and to ensure reasonable utilization of the flying bent so that the build up of dead and uneaten herbage is delayed. Several small fires, well distributed over the areas selected for burning according to a flying bent rotation, are much more to be desired than a single large fire. Where enough green hill is available to supply most of the feed during April–July, mixtures of flying bent and heather should be burnt to encourage heather dominance. (See p. 21).

Summary of the main differences between the management of heather and grass fires

(a) *Length of rotation*

The heather rotation is related to the time taken for heather to reach the appropriate stand condition for burning. It will rarely be less than 7–8 years and on hard ground may be 15–20 years. Grass communities usually accumulate sufficient uneaten dead herbage to require burning every 3–4 years.

(b) *Proportion of the grazing burned*

(i) Heather. The proportion which should be burned each year is dictated by the average time taken for a stand to reach the necessary condition for burning, i.e. the length of rotation. Failure to burn the right proportion allows much of the heather to become too old to be of much use as stock feed. The risks of over-hot fires, losing control of the fire, and poor or slow regeneration after burning are also increased. If too small a proportion is burned, sheep will congregate on the limited areas of regenerating heather and graze them so intensively that the heather may be badly damaged or destroyed, and subsequently replaced by unwanted grasses.

25

(ii) Grass. The proportion burned each year should relate to the subsequent stocking rate, so as to ensure good grazing of the newly burned patches.

(iii) Where the heft system is practised on either heather or grass moors, the proportion of a heft area burned in any year should ensure that the rake of a sheep includes stands of varying age.

(c) *Responses of plants to fire and grazing*

Heather is less fire resistane than flying bent and mat-grass. It is also less able to withstand high levels of grazing use than grasses. Frequent burning and heavy grazing both favour the growth of grasses at the expense of heather.

Sites demanding extra care and attention when burning

1. *Steep slopes.* Where slopes are so steep that disturbing the vegetation could result in risk of erosion, burning, if practised at all, should be done with extra care. Burning should not take place on scree slopes (Photo 6). Fierce updraughts can occur when burning below rocky cliffs and crags and in dry weather this may result in the destruction of trees, bushes and cliff ledge vegetation of conservation interest (see Chapter X). Areas in which this danger exists should be avoided. Where burning is practised on steep slopes small fires may seem sensible from the point of view of reducing the area at risk, but this may attract undue grazing pressure which defeats the aim of minimising disturbance to the vegetation. Where the heather is young the fire should be large enough, or composed of many small fires, so that the proportion burned is sufficient to ensure low grazing pressures. Where the heather is old it is probably best to avoid burning altogether. Regeneration is slow after the fire, and such terrain is exposed to severe damage by torrential rains, etc. These areas should be protected by fire-breaks.

2. *High altitude or exposed sites.* These include all areas around and above the natural altitudinal limit of forest (about 600 m, 2,000 ft. in the east, and lower in the west), steep slopes and bluffs at lesser altitudes, and exposed coastal sites. In these locations growth is slow and the vegetation cover often discontinuous. In general such sites should not be burned. The frequent high winds usually cause heather stems to lie at an angle to the ground and when these are covered with blown soil and detritus the process of layering occurs, i.e. adventitious roots are produced. In this way the vegetation is maintained at an even developmental stage.

3. *Woodland and scrub.* Burning can destroy areas of woodland and scrub both by the direct action of fire on the trees and bushes and by preventing natural regeneration. Fires in the vicinity of such areas should be managed

with care. Woodland and scrub often add to the amenity of an area, they have intrinsic interest for conservation deriving from special plant and animal associations, and they also provide useful shelter.

4. *Peat bog and "flow ground".** Burning of these areas is required only when they are used for grazing purposes. Stocking densities are usually low, and in some cases there is rather little to be gained by burning. Heather, if present, is slow to regenerate and gives place to less useful plants such as deer sedge or cotton sedge. Burning should be restricted to the minimum necessary to meet the needs of stock, especially in areas of value for nature conservation purposes where damage may be caused to the distinctive fauna and flora (see Chapter X).

5. *Large areas of old rank heather.* Regeneration of shoots from the old stem bases will be poor and much of the heather seed may be destroyed in the fire which will be hotter than with younger heather. Such areas should first be divided up with long narrow fires and subsequent burning should be narrow strips between these firebreaks. The strips should be narrow so that the perimeter is large in relation to the total burned area. This is because regeneration may be largely dependent on seed shed into the perimeter by the adjacent older heather.

*"Flow-ground" corresponds most closely to wet moor with cross-leaved heath. See Section V, pages 9–11.

IX

Control of Fires

Good muirburn practice requires adequate control of the fire to ensure that its extent conforms to the plan and purpose of burning, and that it does not escape on to adjoining land. In addition to any risk of damage to neighbouring property, uncontrolled burning cannot follow the principles set out in preceding Chapters, and may lead to undesired changes in the vegetation and habitat.

The differing purposes of burning require differing attitudes to control. A keeper burning for grouse is concerned to create a series of relatively small burnt strips, while avoiding large scale destruction of the heather resource. His need is for fairly rapid progress in terms of area covered, but there is flexibility as regards location and direction of burning. A farmer burning for grazing stock has rather greater freedom of action, but should avoid burning too much of the grazing area in one year. A forester burning a protective fire trace on a plantation boundary must prevent the fire entering the plantation, but will also be concerned that it should not escape on to adjoining land. In this instance, the need is for fairly rapid forward progress on a narrow front, within rather precise limits.

The forester or keeper engaging in muirburn will normally have access to adequate resources of men and equipment and would expect to have firm control over the operation. The upland farmer will usually have relatively few men at this disposal, but where his land adjoins a grouse moor or forest he may not unreasonably expect some degree of help and co-operation from his neighbour to enable him to carry out his burning programme without risk to that neighbour's property. In this situation, however, he may not have full control of the men involved unless there is a clear understanding as to who is in command.

Planning the burn

The location and extent of burning proposed should be clearly defined in the mind of the controller well before the event. He should walk the ground in advance to identify fire-breaks and to estimate their probable effectiveness; he should also locate areas where the fire is likely to speed up or slow down. He should decide the range of weather conditions suitable for his purpose and should have alternative burning patterns in mind to suit these. The use of a map and notebook can be of considerable assistance. Given this degree of forward planning, it is possible to determine the need for additional fire-breaks, and to have some idea of the critical points in the plan if there should be a sudden shift in wind direction or speed.

Climatic conditions in Scotland are such that really good years for muirburn are infrequent—perhaps one year in five on average. However, there are few years when it is impossible to undertake some muirburn. Without prior planning the man with slender resources is likely in average years to miss the short periods of suitable weather and tends in good years to start burning relatively late in long spells of good weather. With prior planning it is possible to start burning as soon as weather conditions are suitable and priority can be given to the burning of fire traces where necessary. If the weather remains suitable the planned programme can be carried out early, so avoiding risk of burning when conditions are becoming critical for safe control.

There may be areas which are particularly dangerous to burn, due to very rank growth or to their proximity to other property. For these areas advance planning is particularly important, since they often require unusual weather conditions if burning is to be carried out safely. In such cases it is sometimes possible to reduce the danger by achieving a partial burn before conditions are judged to be dry enough for normal burning.

The pattern and method of burning differs according to the land use of the area, but burning in successive years can be planned to ease the problems of control in future years. A random pattern of burning dictated by convenience or immediate need is irrational and unsafe.

Conduct of muirburn

There are two main methods of controlled burning which are reasonably safe if directed by experienced men in a sensible manner.

(a) The safest method is to permit the fire front to spread in a pre-determined direction, while extinguishing the flanks of the fire at a desired width. Preferably one or both flanks of the fire should be defined by a natural or prepared fire-break. The rate of forward spread is never allowed to exceed the capability of the working party to extinguish the front quickly.

29

Clearly, the wider the fire front, the greater the danger of the fire getting out of control. This danger is particularly acute under variable conditions and the controller should not hesitate to stop the fire at intervals to re-assess the situation before proceeding.

This method is relatively slow in terms of area covered and expensive in terms of labour input. It is most suitable for creating fire-breaks and producing the narrow burnt strips appropriate in grouse moor management, where the presence of areas previously burnt makes control easier.

(b) The alternative method is to select or prepare fire-breaks surrounding and enclosing the area to be burned, and to start a series of fires around the edge with the intention of allowing them to merge within the area. This technique can be highly effective, but is also very susceptible to error if the fire-breaks are ineffective under the prevailing conditions or become so if conditions change during burning. Being economical in time and effort, it is used to burn off large areas, but there is a temptation to carry out burning of this type under rather extreme conditions in order to achieve a complete burn, despite the attendant disadvantages of a very hot fire (p. 17). The key to success lies in the selection and prior preparation of fire-breaks, and in limiting the size of the fire to ensure that the number of men available can cover the perimeter adequately.

Controlling the rate of spread

The ability of a work party to control a fire depends upon their number, the tools available and the location and quality of fire-breaks. Temporary loss of control may be acceptable, if the fire front is contained by effective fire-breaks. However, the effectiveness of any fire-break diminishes as the rate of fire spread increases. For example, a stream 2 m (6 ft.) wide may be sufficient to stop a fire under light wind conditions, but totally ineffective if the wind speed is doubled. Any planned burn therefore which relies for control solely upon the effectiveness of fire-breaks is always potentially more hazardous than a burn limited mainly by the efforts of men on the ground.

The width of fire front which can be controlled by one man depends on the rate of fire spread. In emergency the man can increase his physical effort and can be re-inforced by other men from points under less stress. However, an active fire front of about 5 m (5–6 yds.) per man allows a good safety margin and is recommended as the maximum which should be permitted. It is also recommended that the total width of fire front should not be allowed to exceed about 55 m (60 yds.), irrespective of the number of men present These limits apply to burning on an open moor. Within "safe" fire-breaks there is much greater latitude. However, special difficulties may be encountered in maintaining control when burning uphill, and wherever possible this should be avoided.

The Forestry Commission and the larger private estates will have supplies of beaters, knapsack sprayers and possibly powered pumps, together with pre-arranged water supplies. The smaller estate or individual farmer will only rarely have spraying equipment or men trained in its use but if available a tractor-drawn sprayer with a powered pump is invaluable. The principal tool in muirburn control is however a simple beater, which can be readily made up from a variety of materials. The traditional tool is the birch broom, made by wiring birch branches on to a springy birch pole some 2 m (6 ft.) long. Other forms of beater have a wire-netting head (Photo 1), or one made of old rubber or even sheet tin, perforated to lessen air resistance. Long-handled shovels are used in some districts while for flying bent an ordinary sack, moistened at intervals to prevent it catching fire, is often preferred.

A lighter tool, which is particularly useful for smothering flames rather than beating them out, is the scraper made from 40 mm aluminium alloy tubing (Photo 2). Its handle, 2–3 m long, is welded on to a head which consists of a frame on to which are bound two or more layers of wire netting, or a perforated sheet of tin.

A reserve supply of beaters and scrapers on the site is essential, as breakages are fairly frequent during use. In addition, it is desirable to have available some knapsack sprayers containing water or a fire-retarding chemical such as mono-ammonium phosphate or sodium alginate. Other important items of equipment are face-masks and gloves, without which the heat may make it impossible to approach and control the fire front.

Fire-breaks

Fire-breaks are a key factor in planning and controlling muirburn. These may be natural features such as a stream, rock face or change of vegetation; or they may be other existing site features such as roads, paths, stone walls or areas of previous burning. Artificial fire-breaks may be created to provide protection on areas where natural features are absent or ineffective as fire barriers. Whatever their form the effectiveness of a fire-break depends upon the conditions at the time. Almost any slight feature can be effective as a start line from which to begin burning, so long as men are present with beaters to check any backward spread of fire. As a stop line for a strong fire front however, a fire-break must be of considerable width before it is safe, unless it is patrolled by men. Semi-permanent artificial fire-breaks are expensive to create and maintain but temporary breaks can often be created cheaply. Such fire-breaks are normally designed to provide a safe start line for subsequent burning rather than to provide an absolute stop line for a major fire.

Fire-breaks can be created by mechanical means such as ploughing to provide a bare earth trace; by using fire or chemical either singly or in combination to provide an area free of vegetation or by combinations of mowing, grazing, fertilizing and re-seeding to create a less inflammable sward.

Assessing the rate of spread

The critical factor in any burning operation is the rate of spread of the fire. To a certain extent measurements of prevailing weather conditions, together with estimates of other factors based on local experience, may be used to predict the ease with which an area may be expected to burn. However, during burning the controller has to rely on his own judgement based on experience. He will be particularly concerned with:

(a) The wind direction and speed, which will only rarely remain constant. Here experience of the probable behaviour of the wind as the day progresses is invaluable. Any significant change in the wind will almost certainly involve a change in fire control tactics. The best conditions are those provided by a steady breeze of about Force 3 on the Beaufort Scale (Table 1). Variable light winds may be dangerous, as are excessively strong and gusty winds. Burning should be started only when the wind is "true" and if conditions change, especially if there is a marked rise in wind speed, it should be stopped as quickly as possible.

(b) Variations in the composition and quantity of the vegetation available for burning. Dense patches of dry material will flare up fiercely, but their presence can often be detected in advance, allowing time for precautions to be taken. Areas of scant vegetation provide useful check lines where a fire can be extinguished readily.

(c) Variations in ground conditions. Fire tends to move more rapidly up-hill, particularly if slope and wind direction coincide, and care is needed when approaching local increases of gradient. Vegetation providing continuous cover on level or smoothly sloping ground will usually burn more rapidly than a broken surface, while the latter may provide the opportunity to break up a hot fire front and facilitate control.

The effect of these factors will be anticipated by the good fire controller, who must be sensitive to any change in conditions if he is to remain "in control" of the situation. Finally, it is important to be sure the fire is properly out before leaving the area.

TABLE 1

Extract from the Specifications and Equivalent Speeds of the Beaufort Scale*

| Force | Description | Specifications for use on land | Equivalent speed at 10 m above ground | | | |
| | | | Knots | | Miles per hour | |
			Mean	Limits	Mean	Limits
0	Calm	Calm; smoke rises vertically.	0	<1	0	<1
1	Light air	Direction of wind shown by smoke drift, but not by wind vanes.	2	1–3	2	1–3
2	Light breeze	Wind felt on face; leaves rustle; ordinary vane moved by wind.	5	4–6	5	4–7
3	Gentle breeze	Leaves and small twigs in constant motion; wind extends light flag.	9	7–10	10	8–12
4	Moderate breeze	Raises dust and loose paper; small branches are moved.	13	11–16	15	13–18
5	Fresh breeze	Small trees in leaf begin to sway; crested wavelets form on inland waters.	19	17–21	21	19–24

* Meteorological Office: The Observer's Handbook (3rd Edition) 1969, Her Majesty's Stationery Office.

X

Muirburn in Relation to Wild-Life

It is true that muirburn causes some reduction in the diversity of the flora and fauna of areas in which it is practised systematically. Its chief aim is, after all, to maintain or improve the productivity of the more useful food plants of upland grazings and sporting lands, by encouraging the dominance of these plants in uniform, even-aged stands. This reduces vegetational diversity and will have a similar effect on animal life.

However, in spite of this these areas still represent an important reservoir of wild plants and animals. On the drier mineral soils herbs such as bluebell,* bitter vetch, bird's-foot trefoil, tormentil, heath bedstraw, devil's bit scabious, common speedwell and violet flourish, whilst on the more peaty soils blaeberry, Scottish cranberry, cloudberry, bog asphodel, milkwort, cross-leaved heath and moorland spotted orchid are among the most frequent plants. There is also a considerable abundance of insect life. The plants and invertebrate animals together constitute sources of food for various larger animals and birds. These include, for example, lizards, adders, frogs and toads, various small rodents, meadow pipits, skylark, stonechat, whinchat, wheatear, and golden plover. Some of these, in turn, contribute to the diet of carnivorous animals, such as the stoat or fox, and birds of prey, for example merlin, raven, buzzard or golden eagle. In terms both of the appeal of the countryside to residents and visitors alike, and of the scientific importance of these plants and animals, they represent a resource of considerable value. It is possible for this resource to be conserved at a reasonable level without interfering with proper management for production from the hills, if the principles of good muirburn practice are strictly followed.

*i.e. the Scottish bluebell or harebell, *Campanula rotundifolia*.

Consequences of bad muirburn practice

Failure to adhere to the principles of good burning practice may adversely affect the wild-life both directly and also indirectly through loss of soil fertility, reduced production or erosion.

For example, continued severe fires may lead to the exposure, alteration or loss of the soil surface. Uncontrolled fires through old stands of heather or flying bent are liable to lead to the destruction of peripheral woodland, mountain pastures, scrub and cliff habitats which should not be burnt at all. These habitats, including screes, rock faces, cliff ledges, ravines and summit areas are often naturally protected from heavy grazing and may have retained their original vegetation, so constituting important refuges for wild-life. The plants and animals are mostly fire-sensitive kinds, such as tall herbs, ferns, trees and shrubs with their dependent populations of invertebrates, birds and other animals. Unreclaimed bogs and fens also contain fire-sensitive plants, while high altitude vegetation is very slow to regenerate. These habitats are therefore also at risk from uncontrolled burning.

Burning outside the legal limits, especially in late spring, is very likely to have damaging consequences to wild-life. Even within the legal period, inadequate fire control may lead to the destruction of nests of certain early-breeding birds (for example, stonechat, raven, snipe, curlew, golden plover, merlin, eagle). A second attempt at breeding may be made but is often less successful, and if maturing young are destroyed in a late fire these birds are unable to nest again. Others will make no second attempt, and late spring fires which are often hotter than normal are fatal to the eggs and young of ground-nesting wading birds such as redshank, greenshank, curlew and dunlin, as well as game birds including red and black grouse and ptarmigan. They will also destroy emerging insects which are normally protected from fire below ground in their winter resting stages.

It is therefore necessary to plan and carry out all burning with great care, to avoid not only damage to wild-life but also deterioration of moorland production. The sensitive scrub, woodland and bog habitats should be protected by natural or artificial fire-breaks. Burning should be directed away from and not towards these features, if necessary dividing the area to be burnt into smaller sections, using small fires lit when it is too damp for a clean burn. Small woods and scrub of natural oak and birch are often valuable components of hill farms, not only for wild-life but also for stock. Mature trees may survive the occasional passage of a fire, but young seedlings and saplings will be killed, and the wood eventually destroyed.

Mires, otherwise known as mosses, bogs or flows, are damaged by muirburning. They have a characteristic structure comprising a pool and hummock pattern, built of layer upon layer of bog moss and sedges. This patterned surface is destroyed and eroded by burning, and of some 10 species of *Sphagnum* moss of which mires are composed, all but two or three are destroyed by normal muirburn practice, with the result that few undamaged examples of the habitat survive with their more sensitive plants. To conserve those examples which remain, these habitats should be excluded from muirburning operations.

The use of fire in management for nature conservation

Moorland managed for nature conservation is best treated so as to produce greater variety in the plant and animal communities. It is possible, by adopting a very long burning cycle (e.g. 30–40 years, or no burning at all if other means are available), to prevent succession to woodland and yet to encourage small-scale patchiness in the vegetation. This develops when heather is allowed to complete its growth cycle and the stand becomes uneven-aged, with young and old plants side by side or separated by gaps. This permits full development of associated plant and animal life, because of the variety of habitat conditions represented in a small area. If, in addition, partial recovery of deeply rooting scrub species, such as juniper, willows and birch, is allowed, both wild-life and soil fertility will be enhanced. The balance between heathland with some scrub development, and a full woodland succession is, however, a fine one and if invading scrub cannot be controlled mechanically, burning is an appropriate control technique, providing fire temperatures can be kept down to levels consistent with successful heather regeneration and soil conservation.

Additional variety in the populations of wild plants and animals is introduced if succession to woodland is encouraged in certain parts of the moor. Here, burning may be used to provide a starting point for the new succession, as it destroys accumulated litter and old vegetation, preparing a suitable seed bed for colonization by tree seedlings. Among native trees and shrubs, birch and Scots pine regenerate well from seed on burnt ground, and on certain soils this applies also to rowan, oak and other broadleaved trees. Many existing pine and birch woods owe their origin to successful colonization following fire. However, tree regeneration is unlikely on areas remote from good seed sources or in the presence of grazing animals. If wild or domestic livestock are present, effective fencing is necessary if fire is to be used to promote tree colonization.

XI

Summary

A recurring theme in this Guide has been the supreme importance of *planning* and *control* in making muirburn. The guidelines for such planning and control have been set out, and the damaging consequences of ignoring these have been indicated.

It is recognised that circumstances vary and it is not always possible to achieve perfection. The most obvious example is seen in wet years, when it is impossible to burn an adequate proportion of the moor. This, however, only makes planning the more important so that in a good year every opportunity can be taken to catch up on a back-log of land over-due for burning, while at the same time avoiding the temptation to take short-cuts by burning excessively large blocks with virtually uncontrolled fires. It cannot be emphasised too strongly that the latter create serious problems for future management and utilization, as well as creating a risk of reduced productivity due to soil damage or the spread of unwanted plants.

With good planning a satisfactory burning policy can generally be achieved over the years, even with rather slender resources. For example, where difficulties are encountered in burning a sufficient proportion of the area in spring, opportunities offered by suitable weather in autumn can be used with great profit, if the farmer or keeper is ready for them in advance. Burning is an effective management technique in maintaining, or even in some cases improving production, and can be prevented from causing undue harm to the environment, but only if the right proportion of the total area is burnt each year, neither too much nor too little, with adequate control so that the fire is neither too hot, yet still gives a good clean burn. No burning is safe if conducted by too few men, while burning under conditions of extreme hazard demonstrates a complete disregard for the interests of others. The main practical details requiring attention may be summarised as follows:

RULES FOR GOOD BURNING

BURNING IS ALLOWED ONLY BETWEEN 1st OCTOBER AND 15th APRIL (unless an extension to 30th April or 15th May has been granted).

1. **Know your area**

   (a) Its climate, and local climatic variations from place to place.
   (b) Its vegetation—the different types, and the amount of each.
   (c) Its terrain—rough and smooth, flats and slopes, variations in altitude.
   (d) Its soils—"hard" and "soft" ground, well drained and poorly drained, amount of peat.
   (e) The grazing use of different parts of the area.
   (f) The expected rate of recovery of vegetation after fire, and the number of years before it is ready for burning again.

2. **Be clear about your burning policy**

   (a) Your ideal rotation (the proportion of the area to be burned each year)
      —fix it in relation to 1(f): e.g. if it is heather and you find it is usually ready for burning at an age of 10 years, aim to burn 1/10 of the total area each year (but not all in one block!).
      —use longer rotations for heather (often between 8 and 15 years), shorter for grass—depending on the size of the sheep flock. Be extra careful where heather is mixed with flying bent, mat-grass or bracken.
   (b) The best size and shape for your burnt areas
      —for grouse, between $\frac{1}{2}$ and 1 ha. (1–2 acres), usually in narrow strips (about 25–30 m wide).
      —for sheep, more variable but much smaller than the rake of a heft.
   (c) The places needing special care, and those which should never be burned (e.g. steep slopes, high ground, exposed ground, woodland or scrub, flow ground).

3. **Plan your programme each year**

   (a) Plan in advance; be ready to use any opportunity. (Remember, in the average season you may have only 20 days or less which are suitable).
   (b) Walk over the area noting the locations to be burnt, size of fires, etc. (Heather is usually ready for burning when it is 20–30 cm; 8–12 in. high).

(c) Identify natural fire-breaks, and note where fire-breaks must be prepared in advance.

(d) Are you up-to-date in your rotation? If not, what extra burning should you allow for in order to catch up?

(e) Calculate the resources you need—men and equipment.

(f) Any special problems? Proximity to neighbour's land or plantations? Patches of very old heather, previously neglected?

(g) Locate your burning with an eye to future management.

4. **Be ready for the burning season**

(a) Make sure you know and stick to the legal dates.

(b) If you are a tenant, remember you are obliged to give your proprietor 28 days' notice in writing of your intention to burn.
If you are a proprietor, prompt response to this notice is always helpful, and any objection must be intimated within 7 days.

(c) Nearer the time, your exact intentions must be made known to your proprietor, as well as to adjoining proprietors and neighbours. They must receive at least 24 hours' notice, and this is especially important if you want to request help (e.g. from the Forestry Commission).

(d) Have adequate equipment ready, and arrangements made to muster men quickly.

(e) Be prepared to use good weather in autumn to start the burning programme.

(f) Make use of weather forecasts.

(g) Start as soon as conditions are right—do not delay until the vegetation becomes tinder dry.

5. **On the day**

(a) Judge carefully if conditions are suitable. Be sure the wind is right, and *be careful under changeable conditions.*

(b) Start burning as soon as conditions are favourable with a steady weather pattern; finish before nightfall.

(c) Restrict the width of the fire front to that which the men can handle.

(d) If conditions change, stop burning and re-assess.

FINALLY, DO NOT:

(a) Burn outside the legal period.

(b) Burn indiscriminately.

(c) Submit to the temptation to burn excessively large blocks in fine weather.

(d) Burn any patch of ground more often than necessary.

(e) Leave preparation to the last minute.

(f) Carry on burning late in the evening.

(g) Allow the fire to escape, especially into wild-life refuges (high land, woods, cliffs, ravines, flow ground).

APPENDIX NO. 1

List of Working Party Members

Chairman:

C. H. GIMINGHAM, B.A., PH.D., F.R.S.E.	Professor of Botany, University of Aberdeen.
MISS S. A. GRANT, B.SC., M.SC.	Plant and Soils Department, Hill Farming Research Organisation, Edinburgh.
M. E. BALL, B.SC.(FOR.)	Deputy Regional Officer (West), Nature Conservancy Council, Inverness.
J. C. CLARK, B.SC.(AGRIC.)	Senior Inspector, Department of Agriculture and Fisheries for Scotland, Edinburgh.
J. EADIE, B.SC.(AGRIC.)	Head of Animal Department, Hill Farming Research Organisation, Edinburgh.
G. D. FINDLAY, B.SC.(AGRIC.)	Area Agricultural Adviser, County Advisory Service, North of Scotland College of Agriculture, Inverness.
D. A. GOODE, B.SC., PH.D.	Chief Scientist's Group, Nature Conservancy Council, Edinburgh.

40

J. B. D. Herriott, B.SC., PH.D.	Crop Production Advisory and Development Department, East of Scotland College of Agriculture, Edinburgh.
A. MacLeod, N.D.A., N.D.D.	Area Adviser, Agricultural Advisory and Development Service, West of Scotland Agricultural College, Oban.
G. R. Miller, B.SC., PH.D.	Institute of Terrestrial Ecology, Banchory.
H. D. Sempill, A.R.I.C.S.	Lands Officer, Department of Agriculture and Fisheries for Scotland, Oban.
G. G. M. Taylor, B.SC.(FOR.)	Assistant Conservator, East Scotland Conservancy, Forestry Commission, Aberdeen.

Secretary

C. O. Badenoch	Assistant Regional Officer (Borders), Nature Conservancy Council, Edinburgh.

APPENDIX NO. 2

Extracts from the Hill Farming Act, 1946 dealing with muirburn (Scotland)

The Hill Farming Act, 1946, which became law on 6th November, 1946, makes provision for the regulation of muirburn in Scotland. The Sections dealing with this subject are quoted below:

Repeal of 16 and 17 Geo.5.c.30.

22. The Heather Burning (Scotland) Act, 1926, is hereby repealed and, in relation to Scotland, the provisions of the five next succeeding sections shall have effect in lieu thereof.

Prohibition of muirburn at certain times.

23.—(1) Subject to the provisions of this section it shall not be lawful to make muirburn except before the sixteenth day of April or after the thirtieth day of September in any year:

41

Provided that it shall be lawful for the proprietor of any lands, or for the tenant with the written authority of the proprietor or of his factor or commissioner, to make muirburn thereon during the period from the sixteenth day to the thirtieth day of April both days inclusive.

(2) In the case of lands more than fifteen hundred feet above sea level the preceding subsection shall have effect as if for the thirtieth day of April there were substituted the fifteenth day of May.

(3) The Secretary of State may in any year, if it appears to him necessary or expedient so to do for the purpose of facilitating the making of muirburn, direct that subsection (1) of this section shall have effect as respects such lands as may be specified in the direction as if for the sixteenth day of April there were substituted such day thereafter as he may deem proper, being a day not later than the first day of May or, in the case of lands more than fifteen hundred feet above sea level, the sixteenth day of May. Any such direction may be given as respects all lands in Scotland, or as respects the lands in any county or any part of a county, or as respects any particular lands or classes of lands.

Notice of the giving of any direction under this subsection (other than a direction given only as respects any particular lands) shall be published in one or more newspapers circulating in the locality in which the lands to which the direction relates are situated.

(4) Any person who makes muirburn or causes or procures the making of muirburn on any lands in contravention of this section shall be guilty of an offence.

Right of tenant to make muirburn notwithstanding terms of lease.

24.—(1) Where the tenant of any land is of the opinion that it is necessary or expedient for the purpose of conserving or improving that land to make muirburn thereon, it shall, subject to the provisions of this Act, be lawful for him to make muirburn therein notwithstanding any provision in the lease of such land prohibiting, whether absolutely or subject to conditions, or restricting in any way, the making of muirburn.

(2) Not less than twenty-eight days before so making muirburn the tenant shall give notice to the proprietor of the land of the places at which, and the approximate extent to which he proposes to make muirburn; and if the proprietor is dissatisfied as to the places at which, or the extent to which the tenant proposes to make muirburn, he shall, within seven days after the receipt of the intimation from the tenant, give notice to the tenant stating the grounds of his dissatisfaction and shall refer the matter to the Secretary of State for his decision, and pending such decision the tenant shall not proceed with the operation of muirburn with respect to which reference has been so made.

(3) On any reference under the foregoing subsection the Secretary of State, after such inquiry as he may think fit, and after considering any representations made by the parties interested, shall give such directions as he may deem proper regulating the muirburn, and it shall thereupon be lawful for the tenant to make muirburn in accordance with the direction. Any direction given by the Secretary of State under this subsection shall be final.

(4) It shall subject to the provisions of this Act be lawful for the tenant of any land, notwithstanding any provision in the lease of such land prohibiting, whether absolutely or subject to conditions, or restricting in any way, the making of muirburn, to make muirburn thereon if the work is done in accordance with an approved hill farming land improvement scheme; and the provisions of subsections (2) and (3) of this section shall not apply to the making of such muirburn.

Regulation of muirburn

25. Any person who—

(*a*) commences to make muirburn between one hour after sunset and one hour before sunrise; or

(*b*) fails to provide at the place where he is about to make muirburn, or to maintain there while he is making muirburn, a sufficient staff and equipment to control and regulate the burning operations so as to prevent damage to any woodlands on or adjoining the land where the operations are taking place or to any adjoining lands, march fences or other subjects; or

(*c*) makes muirburn on any land without having given to the proprietor of the lands or woodlands adjoining the land and, if he is a tenant to the proprietor of the land, not less than twenty-four hours' notice of his intention to make muirburn and of the day on which, the places at which and the approximate extent to which, he intends to make muirburn; or

(*d*) makes muirburn on any land without due care so as to cause damage to any woodlands on or adjoining the land or any adjoining lands, woodlands, march fences or other subjects,

shall be guilty of an offence.

Notices as to muirburn

26.—(1) Any notice required to be given under either of the two last preceding sections shall be given in writing.

(2) Any notice so required to be given to a proprietor shall be deemed to be given to the proprietor if it is given to his factor, commissioner or other local representative.

Offences as to muirburn

27. Any person guilty of an offence against section twenty-three or section twenty-five of this Act shall be liable on summary conviction to a fine not exceeding five pounds or to imprisonment for a term not exceeding thirty days or to both such fine and such imprisonment.

*   *   *

Provisions as to Scotland

39.—(1) This Act shall, in its application to Scotland, have effect subject to the following modifications:—

*   *   *

(*f*) unless the context otherwise requires, the following expressions shall have the meanings hereby assigned to them respectively, that is to say:—

"lease" in relation to a common pasture or grazing includes regulations made or approved by the Land Court under the Small Landholders (Scotland) Acts, 1886 to 1931;

"making muirburn" includes setting fire to or burning any heath or muir; and

"tenant" means a tenant for agricultural or pastoral purposes, and, in the case of a common pasture or grazing, includes the committee appointed under the Small Landholders (Scotland) Acts, 1886 to 1931.

APPENDIX NO. 3

A Short Bibliography

There is extensive literature on muirburn although much of it concentrates on management of heather-dominated lands and less has been written about grass-dominated areas. Further information relating to many of the subjects treated in the Guide can be obtained in the following:—

Gimingham, C. H. (1972). *Ecology of Heathlands*. London, Chapman and Hall.

Leslie, A. S. (Editor) (1911). *The Grouse in Health and Disease*. London, Smith, Elder and Co.

Watson, A. and Miller, G. R. (1976). *Grouse Management* (revised edition). The Game Conservancy, Booklet 12, Fordingbridge.

Scottish Home and Health Department (1972). *Fire Protection for Forests and Woodlands*. HMSO (also Home Office publication, undated, of the same name).

Symposium on Land Use in the Scottish Highlands. "Advancement of Science". Vol. 21, 1964.

Acts of Parliament affecting the making or results of Muirburn:—

Hill Farming Act, 1946

    i) Muirburn (Scotland).

    ii) Regulations (England and Wales): The Burning of Heather and Grass.

Agriculture Act, 1958. (Burning of Heather and Grass, England and Wales).

Clean Air Acts, 1956 and 1968.

Town and Country Planning (Scotland) Act, 1972.

Printed in Scotland for Her Majesty's Stationery Office by David J. Clark Limited, Glasgow.

Dd 403658/3687 Gp 221 K 12 2/77